THE TOP TEN
LEADERS
THAT CHANGED THE WORLD

Anita Ganeri

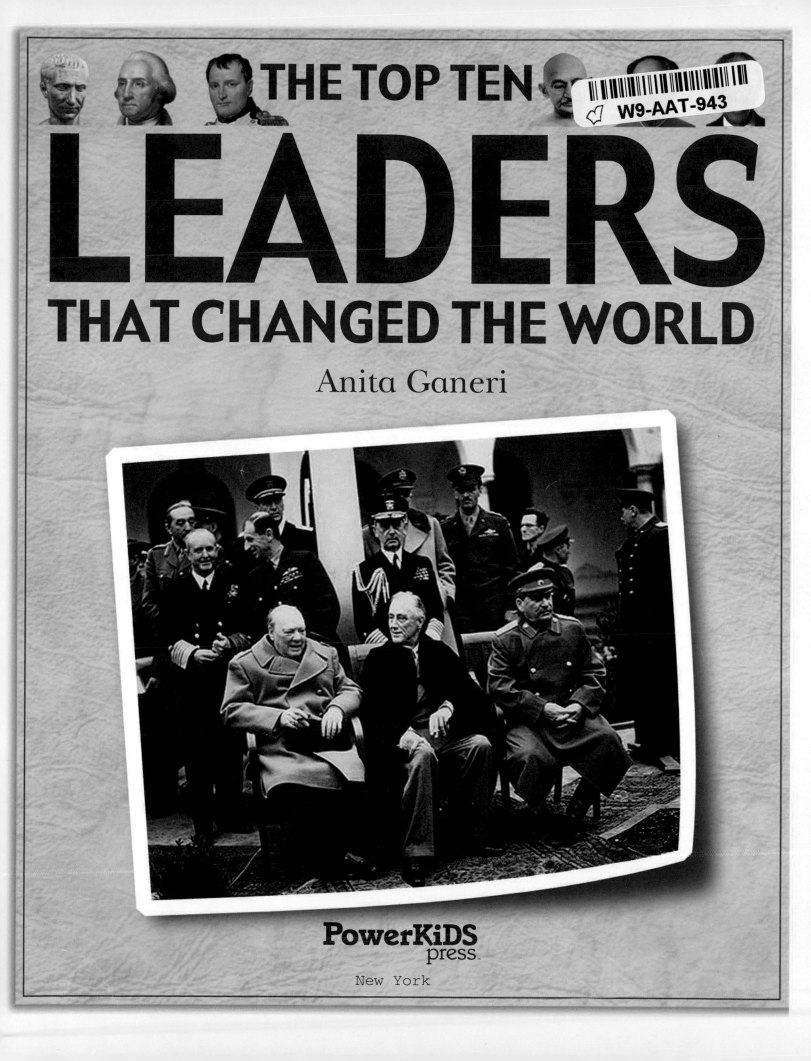

PowerKiDS press

New York

Published in 2010 by The Rosen Publishing Group, Inc.
29 East 21st Street, New York 10010

Designed and produced by
David West Books

Designer: David West
Illustrator: David West
Editor: Katharine Pethick
U.S. Editor: Kara Murray

Photographic credits: 19bl, eurok; 19br, jiashiang; 22tl, p_c_w; 23tl, Paul Mannixj

Library of Congress Cataloging-in-Publication Data

Ganeri, Anita, 1961–
The top ten leaders that changed the world / Anita Ganeri.
p. cm. — (Top ten)
Includes index.
ISBN 978-1-4358-9164-7 (library binding) — ISBN 978-1-4358-9165-4 (pbk.) —
ISBN 978-1-4358-9166-1 (6-pack)
1. Leadership—Case studies—Juvenile literature. 2. Political leadership—Case studies—Juvenile literature. 3. Social change—Case studies—Juvenile literature. 4. Politicians—Biography—Juvenile literature. 5. Social reformers—Biography—Juvenile literature. 6. Biography—Juvenile literature. 7. World history—Juvenile literature. I. Title.
HM1261.G36 2010
909.09'9—dc22
[B]
2009021301

Contents

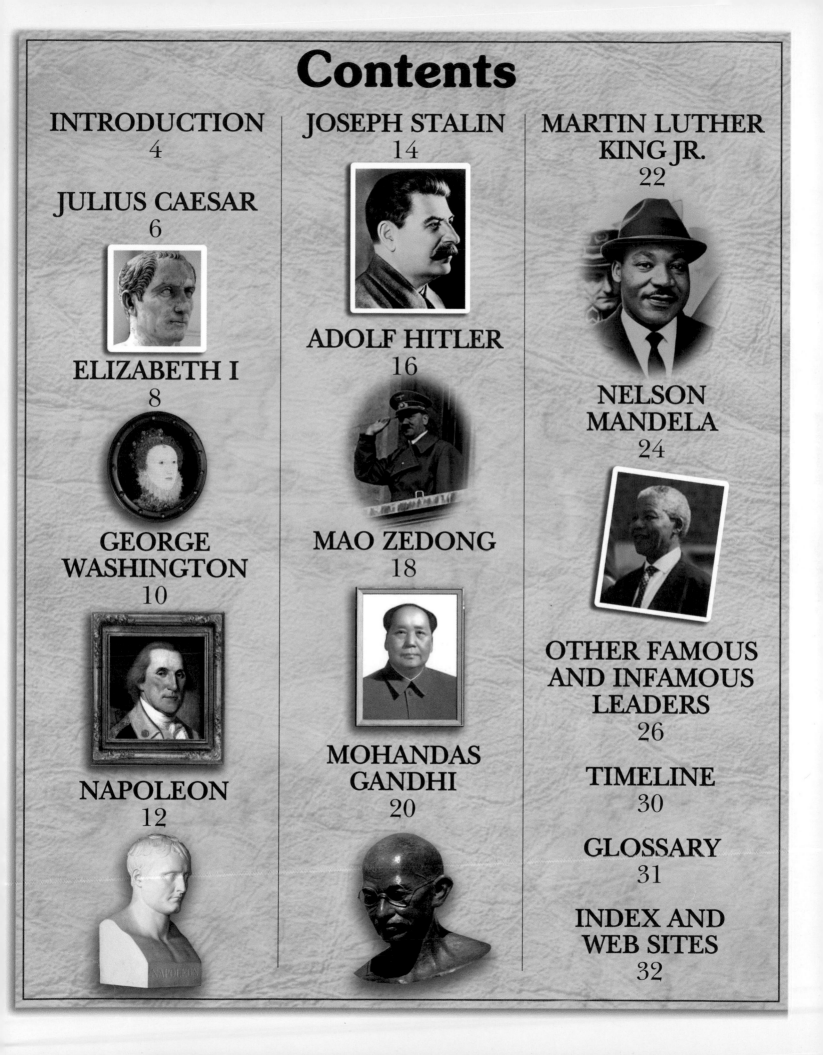

Introduction

The following leaders have been selected as the top ten that have most changed our world, for better or for worse. Why have these ten leaders made it and not others?

✱ First, we have chosen to focus on social and political leaders, rather than religious leaders.

Although they are important to many people, religious leaders, such as the Buddha, are not included in the list.

Some famous leaders from the past, like Cleopatra (shown here welcoming Julius Caesar), were important in their day but have not affected the modern world.

✱ Second, the leader must have inspired or affected the whole world, not just a part of it.

4

✳ Third, the effects of his or her leadership must still be felt today.

You might disagree with the people that have been chosen. In that case, you might want to put together your own list.

Alexander the Great conquered a vast empire, but his influence was felt most strongly around the Mediterranean and in the Middle East.

Julius Caesar (100 BC–44 BC)

Julius Caesar was born in Rome at a time when rival Roman armies were fighting for power. Because he was part of an influential political family, he left Rome in 82 BC in fear of his life. However, he returned in 73 BC and entered politics. Caesar spent two years as governor of Spain (then a Roman province), and then became governor of Gaul (in modern-day France). He stayed in Gaul for nearly ten years, leading military campaigns. In 53 BC, Pompey, a Roman noble who feared Caesar's power, became leader of the Senate. He ordered Caesar to return to Rome, but Caesar refused.

In 49 BC, with a legion of loyal soldiers, Caesar crossed the River Rubicon, which marked the northern boundary of Italy, triggering a civil war. Then, Caesar's army marched south toward Rome.

Rome's territories 44 BC

Roman Empire, third century AD

The map shows how, following Caesar's conquests, Rome expanded to dominate Europe and the Middle East right up until the fifth century.

The Gaulish leader Vercingetorix surrendered to Caesar at the Battle of Alesia.

MASTER OF ROME

Within a few months, Caesar had military control of Italy. However, it took him four years to defeat Pompey and subdue all the far-flung Roman provinces. Caesar finally returned to Rome in 45 BC and was made dictator for life by the Senate. He made improvements to the tax system, the legal system, and the Senate. He also settled Rome's debts. However, Rome was a republic, run by the people, and some senators thought Caesar was becoming too powerful. They hatched a plot to kill him, and Caesar was assassinated in March 44 BC. Although he was assassinated, Caesar's conquests and strong leadership established Rome as a powerful empire for centuries after his death. He was a brilliant speaker in the Roman Senate and a master tactician on the battlefield. Apart from being a great leader, Caesar is also remembered for his reform of the calendar, known as the Julian calendar.

The title of the emperors of the German Empire was Kaiser, after Caesar's name.

The Julian calendar remained in use into the 20th century as a national calendar in some countries, but generally it has been replaced by the modern Gregorian calendar.

Elizabeth I (1533–1603)

"I know I have the body of a weak and feeble woman; but I have the heart and stomach of a king," said Queen Elizabeth I in 1588, as she rallied troops gathered to fight off an imminent Spanish invasion. The daughter of Henry VIII of England and his second wife, Anne Boleyn, Elizabeth was raised as a Protestant at a time when Protestants and Catholics were at war with each other. During the reign of her Catholic half sister, Mary, she was put under house arrest for many years. When Mary died in 1558, however, Elizabeth became queen. In 1588, Philip of Spain sent a huge fleet of ships, called the Armada, to destroy the English navy and put a Catholic ruler on the throne. However, the invasion never arrived since the Armada had already been stopped by the English fleet.

During the Battle of Gravelines, the English fleet crushed the Spanish Armada.

Elizabeth I rallied her troops at Tilbury, on the River Thames.

GOOD QUEEN BESS

The defeat of the Spanish Armada was followed by celebrations throughout England. The victory confirmed Elizabeth's popularity with her people, who called her Good Queen Bess. Elizabeth proved to be a wise leader. She relied on a group of important advisors called the Privy Council but used her own judgment of character to manage the rivalry between the powerful English aristocrats. Elizabeth also encouraged her seafaring adventurers, such as Sir Francis Drake and Sir Walter Raleigh, to explore new lands and raid Spanish ships to fill the country's treasury.

Under Elizabeth, England became an important Protestant nation in Europe for the first time.

Although Raleigh's settlement at Roanoke Island, off the coast of what is now North Carolina, ended in failure, it paved the way for later colonies. In 1600, Elizabeth granted a royal charter to the East India Company, which began trading with China and India. These were the beginnings of a British Empire that would change the world.

The Elizabethan period in history saw a huge leap in exploration. Elizabeth financed explorers like Drake, who managed to circumnavigate the globe.

George Washington (1732–1799)

On Christmas night in 1776, George Washington led the troops of his Continental Army across the icy Delaware River in New Jersey to launch a surprise attack on British forces at Trenton. It was just one of the victories for the Continental Army during the American Revolution. Washington was born into a rich farming family in Virginia. In his 20s, he gained valuable military experience in the Seven Years' War against French colonists. In the 1770s, disagreements between the colonists and the British government over unfair taxes and governance without representation led to the American Revolution. The war began in 1775. By then, Washington had become a leading political figure and was made commander in chief of the colonial military forces. He formed the Continental Army and prepared to begin the fight for independence.

Washington at his family farm in Mount Vernon, Virginia

AMERICAN INDEPENDENCE

In 1776, the colonists declared independence from Great Britain, creating the United States of America. Washington's Continental Army gradually gained the upper hand against the British, finally winning the war at the Battle of Yorktown in 1781. Washington then returned to his Virginia farm. However, he was persuaded to lead the writing of the U.S. Constitution in 1787 and, in 1789, was elected the first president of the United States. He was reelected in 1792 and served until 1797. Then he finally retired to his farm, where he died two years later. Washington, the most famous founding father, led America from a collection of colonies to a new, independent nation that has became the superpower of today.

A dollar coin featuring Washington

Washington resigned from leading the army after the American Revolution.

Washington is commemorated in street and building names all across America, including the Washington Monument, which is the world's tallest obelisk.

11

Napoleon (1769–1821)

In October 1795, during the French Revolution, troops loyal to the royal family marched into Paris, aiming to regain control of France from the republican government. A young general, Napoleon Bonaparte, took command of the seriously outnumbered republican forces. Under Napoleon's leadership, they stopped the royalists in their tracks. This small but decisive battle became known as 13 Vendémiaire, after its date in the French Revolutionary calendar. It saved the republican government and made Napoleon a national hero.

Napoleon had joined the army as an artillery officer at the age of 16 and had risen quickly through the ranks. His first military success was a victory over French antirepublican and British forces at Toulon in 1793. By 1796, he had control of the French army in Italy. Over the next few years, he led victories for France over Austria and conquered Egypt.

Bonaparte made himself Emperor Napoleon I of France at his coronation at the Notre Dame Cathedral in Paris.

EMPEROR OF FRANCE

In 1799, Napoleon returned to France from Egypt, overthrew the republican government, and took charge. Five years later, he proclaimed himself emperor of France and began expanding the French Empire with military campaigns in eastern Europe, Spain, and Italy. At home, he changed the French laws to give the people better rights. These laws were called the Napoleonic Code. But after a failed attempt to invade Russia in 1812, his empire collapsed. Napoleon was exiled to the island of Elba but managed to escape and seize power again. Among others, Britain, Austria, and Prussia decided to invade France to stop him. Napoleon led an army to face them but was defeated at the Battle of Waterloo in Belgium. Again he was exiled, this time to the remote island of St. Helena in the Atlantic Ocean, where he died six years later. Napoleon is famous for being a military leader, but his legacy also includes the Napoleonic Code. With its emphasis on clearly written and accessible laws, the code strongly influenced laws around the world.

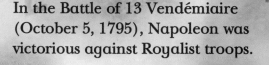

In the Battle of 13 Vendémiaire (October 5, 1795), Napoleon was victorious against Royalist troops.

A British cartoon showing Napoleon being exiled to Elba

The 1815 Battle of Waterloo was a disaster for Napoleon.

Joseph Stalin (1878–1953)

In 1894, the teenage Joseph Stalin began studies at a theological college. However, he abandoned theology when he heard about the political ideas of German philosopher Karl Marx from his fellow students. Stalin decided to support the revolution against the Russian monarchy and joined a communist group called the Bolsheviks. He organized bank robberies, kidnappings, and other illegal activities to raise money for the group. Stalin was arrested several times, imprisoned, and exiled to Siberia, but he quickly became a major figure in the Bolshevik movement. In 1917, the Russian Revolution began during World War I. The Russian monarchy was overthrown, and Stalin was released from prison. After a civil war, the Bolsheviks took power. In 1922, the Soviet Union was formed. That same year, Stalin was elected general secretary of the Communist Party. From this extremely powerful position, Stalin eliminated his political opponents to become outright leader of the Soviet Union.

RUTHLESS TACTICS

Stalin was deeply suspicious of his political rivals and ruthlessly eliminated them. Millions were executed or sent to labor camps in a reign of terror known as the Great Purge. In 1941, Hitler

Armed Bolsheviks in the revolution of 1917

Russia's soldiers answered Stalin's call to defend the city that bore his name, Stalingrad, in 1942.

launched an invasion of the Soviet Union. Rallied by Stalin, the Red Army eventually drove the Germans back, but tens of millions of Russians died. When Germany was defeated in 1945, the Soviets controlled most of eastern Europe. To keep power, Stalin made sure his neighboring countries were run by Communist governments. Stalin was

"The big three," Winston Churchill, Franklin D. Roosevelt, and Stalin, met in 1945 to decide the future of Europe.

a ruthless leader and often used brutal methods. Under his leadership, the Soviet Union emerged as an industrial and military power that dominated eastern Europe for decades. After he died, Stalin was denounced, beginning the period known as de-Stalinization.

Stalin led many political rallies for the Bolsheviks.

Ruthless and determined, Stalin was a powerful personality and leader.

Adolf Hitler (1889–1945)

In 1939, German leader Adolf Hitler invaded Poland, and World War II began. Germany soon controlled most of Europe, and in 1941, as part of his plan for world domination, Hitler ordered an attack on Russia. Born in Austria, Hitler fought for Germany in World War I. In 1920, he joined the National Socialist German Workers' Party (the Nazis), aiming to regain Germany's power after its defeat in World War I. The party was fiercely anti-Semitic and anti-Communist. In 1921, the power-hungry Hitler became party leader. In 1933, as German chancellor, he quickly took total control of the country, making himself dictator. Soon, he was ready to put his master plan into action.

Here Hitler is shown speaking in the Reichstag (German parliament) in 1941.

MASS MURDER IN EUROPE

Hitler's domination of Europe did not last, and by 1945, his forces were in retreat. As the Soviet Red Army reached the outskirts of Berlin, Hitler killed himself. He and his forces had committed appalling acts before and during the war, killing millions of people considered by Hitler to be inferior, including an estimated six million Jews. At the end of World War II, the political map of Europe changed radically. Eventually, Germany was divided in two, and so was the world. The Soviets dominated the East and the other Allies, including the United States and Britain, dominated the West. This situation eventually led to the cold war. Hitler was responsible for plunging the entire globe into a war that, when over, resulted in a world divided into East and West.

Auschwitz extermination camp

THE STARS AND STRIPES

HITLER DEAD

Fuehrer Fell at CP, German Radio Says; Doenitz at Helm, Vows War Will Continue

Churchill Hints Peace Is at Hand

Modern-day neo-Nazis are another of Hitler's shameful legacies.

Hemmed in by Allied and Russian forces, Hitler took his own life.

Mao Zedong (1893–1976)

Mao Zedong became interested in communism while working at Beijing University in 1918. In 1921, he visited Shanghai, where he helped start the Chinese Communist Party. The party's aim was to revolt against traditional Chinese society, transferring power to the peasants. Six years later, the Kuomintang, the Communists' rivals, seized power and civil war broke out. Forced south into a region called Jiangxi, the Communists later set up their own government, with Mao as its leader. Mao gradually built up an army, known as the Red Army. In 1933, the Kuomintang attacked and pushed the Red Army to the brink of defeat.

To escape, Mao led the Red Army on a 6,000-mile (9,600 km) journey north to safety. Known as the Long March, it was a treacherous journey. Of the 100,000 who set out, just 20,000 arrived at the end.

Mao fought in the revolution of 1911, which toppled the last emperor of China.

CULTURAL REVOLUTION

After World War II, civil war broke out again in China. This time, the Communists gradually got the upper hand and, in 1949, the People's Republic of China was founded, with Mao as its chairman. Now Mao could start his revolution in earnest. He made changes, such as building new roads and power plants, and confiscated farms from landlords and gave them to the peasants. In 1958, Mao planned his "Great Leap Forward," ordering rural communities to grow all their own food. However, the plan failed badly. Millions of Chinese died in famines and, in 1959, Mao resigned. He returned to power in 1966 to launch the Cultural Revolution, which threatened anyone, especially intellectuals, who disagreed with his ideas. Mao remained president until his death in 1976. By founding the People's Republic of China, Mao paved the way for the country to become the world superpower it is today.

Mao and President Richard Nixon in 1972

Mao shown with Joseph Stalin on a Soviet poster

The *Sayings of Chairman Mao*, also known as *The Little Red Book*

Mao's influence is like that of Qin, the emperor who unifed China in the third century BC (see page 26).

Mohandas Gandhi (1869–1948)

Mohandas Gandhi was born in India in 1869. India was part of the British Empire at that time. After studying in London, Gandhi practiced law in South Africa. He was appalled at the way Indian workers were treated and encouraged nonviolent protest, which he called *satyagraha* or "force of truth." In 1915, Gandhi returned to India and, from 1919, led the Indian campaign for independence from Britain. He encouraged boycotting British goods and civil disobedience. In 1930, the British wouldn't allow others to make and sell salt, a vital part of the Indian diet. In protest, Gandhi led a "Salt March" to the sea, resulting in a change to the law.

Gandhi as a young lawyer in South Africa in 1900

FORCE OF TRUTH

In 1944, the British agreed to grant India independence. However, many Indian Muslims wanted a separate country for themselves, leaving India for the majority Hindus. Gandhi was against this, as he thought that all Indians, regardless of religion, should be able to live together. In 1947, India finally became independent, but parts of it were split off to create Muslim Pakistan. Partition, as this split was called, caused violent riots during which hundreds of thousands of people were displaced or died. Deeply distressed, Gandhi protested by fasting, an action that eventually stopped the fighting. In 1948, Gandhi was assassinated by a Hindu extremist. His use of nonviolent protest helped lead India to independence and made him an influential figure for other protest leaders such as Martin Luther King Jr. and Nelson Mandela.

The partition of India led to the mass relocation of Hindu and Muslim Indians.

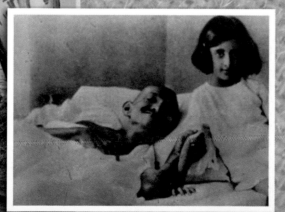

Gandhi fasting in 1924. Gandhi used fasting as a political tool in the 1940s.

Gandhi with Lord Mountbatten, the last viceroy of India

Martin Luther King Jr. (1929–1968)

"I have a dream," proclaimed Martin Luther King Jr., "that my four little children will one day live in a nation where they will not be judged by the color of their skin but by the content of their character." These words were part of King's famous speech at a 1963 civil rights demonstration in Washington, D.C. At that time, there was still racial segregation in some states, which kept black and white people separate from one another in many situations. An African American, King became a clergyman in 1954. In 1955, he led a successful bus boycott in Montgomery, Alabama, where black people were forced to sit at the back of buses. Many more nonviolent protests followed. The protesters were often attacked by white extremists, and King's home was bombed. Often King and the protesters were arrested.

THE DREAM FULFILLED

Under Martin Luther King's leadership, the civil rights movement helped change American society. The Civil Rights Act of 1964 outlawed segregation and racial discrimination, and in the same year, Martin Luther King was awarded the Nobel Peace Prize. King continued to protest for voting rights and better conditions for black people.

Then, in 1968, tragedy struck when King was assassinated in Memphis, Tennessee. By helping to gain equal rights for African Americans and showing that injustices could be righted by nonviolent protest, Martin Luther King is regarded as one of the top ten leaders who changed the world.

A segregated drinking fountain in North Carolina in the 1930s

The march on Washington was a monumental event.

King's many achievements have inspired leaders like President Barack Obama.

White Americans are shown here protesting the racial integration of schools in 1959.

23

Nelson Mandela (BORN 1918)

In 1948, the white National Party came to power in South Africa. It introduced a system of unfair laws, known as apartheid, which forced black people and other minorities to live apart from whites and banned them from holding important jobs. It also introduced new "pass laws," forcing black people to carry identity papers at all times. Nelson Mandela, a lawyer, was a member of the African National Congress (ANC), which campaigned for civil rights for black people. In 1952, Mandela became ANC deputy president and took part in nonviolent demonstrations against apartheid. In 1960, during protests against the pass laws, 69 demonstrators were killed by the police. Reluctantly, Mandela set up an armed section of the ANC that carried out acts of sabotage against the government. In 1962, Mandela was arrested, convicted of treason, and sentenced to life in prison.

Mandela's prison cell on Robben Island. Below, Mandela sits and sews prison clothes in the yard of Robben Island prison.

RAINBOW NATION

From prison, Mandela secretly kept in contact with his ANC colleagues and wrote most of his autobiography. He also remained the figurehead of the antiapartheid movement. During the 1980s, international pressure on South Africa to free Mandela grew. He was finally released in 1990, after 27 years in prison and became leader of the ANC. With South African president F. W. de Klerk, he negotiated the end of apartheid and was jointly awarded the Nobel Peace Prize. After the country's first free elections in 1994, Mandela was sworn in as president of South Africa. He remained president until 1999. More than any other person, Mandela helped lead South Africa from being a segregated country to a multiracial democracy and is seen as an influential leader in the fight for racial equality throughout the world.

FOR USE BY WHITE PERSONS

THESE PUBLIC PREMISES AND THE AMENITIES THEREOF HAVE BEEN RESERVED FOR THE EXCLUSIVE USE OF WHITE PERSONS.

By Order Provincial Secretary

VIR GEBRUIK DEUR BLANKES

HIERDIE OPENBARE PERSEEL EN DIE GERIEWE DAARVAN IS VIR DIE UITSLUITLIKE GEBRUIK VAN BLANKES AANGEWYS.

Op Las Provinsiale Sekretaris

An apartheid sign

A 1986 concert in support of freeing Nelson Mandela

Mandela with President Bill Clinton in 1993, one year before he became president of South Africa

Other Famous and Infamous Leaders

EMPEROR QIN (259–210 BC)

In 221 BC, Qin Shi Huangdi, ruler of the Qin dynasty, proclaimed himself the first emperor of China and gave his name to the country. A powerful and ruthless ruler, Qin abolished the system of local states and established a strong central government. He also standardized the country's script, laws, currency, and system of weights and measures. Until then, each state had had its own systems, which made things very confusing. Qin also ordered the building of the Great Wall of China, to keep out hostile invaders from the north. The emperor died in 210 BC, aged just 49. His extraordinary tomb was guarded by an army of thousands of life-sized clay warriors, called the Terra-Cotta Army.

The famous Terra-Cotta Army was rediscovered in 1974.

GENGHIS KHAN (ca. 1162–1227)

Genghis Khan, a Mongol leader, was a soldier and politician whose armies conquered the largest land empire in history. The Mongols were nomadic horsemen from Mongolia who were originally split into warring tribes. When his father died, Genghis, then named Temuchin, became chief of one of the tribes at the age of 13. He soon began to build a powerful army to gain control over his neighbors. By 1206, he had become ruler of Mongolia and was given the title Genghis Khan, meaning "universal ruler." His armies then swept through central Asia, ruthlessly killing anyone who blocked their path. In 1225, Genghis proceeded with his conquest of China, completed after his death by his grandson, Kublai Khan.

This statue in Mongolia commemorates Genghis Khan.

PETER THE GREAT (1672–1725)

Peter I of Russia

As a young man, in 1695, Peter I led a force against the Ottoman Empire. He later toured Europe to win allies in Russia's fight against the Ottomans. From 1700 to 1721, Peter I led Russia's newly improved army and navy in a successful war against Sweden, then the leading power in northern Europe. This, and other foreign conquests, greatly increased Russia's political importance and helped expand its trade. Peter I went on to reform the government, start Russia's first newspaper, and found schools, museums, and art galleries. In 1703, he built the city of St. Petersburg and made it his capital. By the time Peter I died in 1725, he had transformed Russia into a great European power.

The battle of Poltava in 1709 was Peter the Great's decisive blow against the powerful Swedes.

ABRAHAM LINCOLN (1809–1865)

Abraham Lincoln was the sixteenth president of the United States. He is considered to be one of the greatest U.S. presidents. Lincoln was elected to Congress in 1846. In 1856, he began campaigning for the Republican Party. He gained attention for his strong antislavery views. In 1860, he was elected president. The following year, 11 Southern states broke away from the Union to form their own Confederacy, triggering the Civil War. As commander in chief, Lincoln steered the Union forces to victory. In 1863, he also announced the freedom of slaves in many parts of the United States, leading the way for the eventual abolition of slavery. The Civil War ended in April 1865, when the Confederate troops surrendered. Five days later, Lincoln was shot by an assassin in Washington, D.C. He died the next day.

Lincoln is famous for saving the United States.

VLADIMIR ILYICH LENIN (1870–1924)

The founder of the Communist Party in Russia, Lenin studied law but became involved in politics and was a follower of Karl Marx. In 1903, he became leader of the Bolsheviks. At that time, Russia was ruled by a royal family. Conditions for ordinary people were very hard and unrest began to grow. In 1917, rioting broke out. With World War I raging, life for most Russian people had gone from bad to

Lenin

worse. Lenin returned from exile and called for the government to be overthrown. In November 1917, the Bolsheviks attacked St. Petersburg and seized power. Lenin became head of the new Communist government and moved the capital to Moscow. After Lenin's death in 1924, his body was preserved and put on public display in Red Square, Moscow.

FRANKLIN D. ROOSEVELT (1882–1945)

Roosevelt was the thirty-second president of the United States, and the only person to be elected four times. His political career began when he was elected to

Roosevelt signs the United States' declaration of war against Germany.

the New York State Senate in 1910. He later served twice as governor of New York. In 1932, he beat Herbert Hoover in the presidential election. Roosevelt led his country brilliantly through two of the greatest crises of the twentieth century. He came to office at the time of the Great Depression, when the United States was suffering mass unemployment and a collapse of its economy. In response, Roosevelt introduced the New Deal, a program of financial support and job creation. Roosevelt's third term in office was dominated by the entry of the United States into World War II.

FDR on the dime

MIKHAIL GORBACHEV (BORN 1931)

After studying law, Mikhail Gorbachev joined the Soviet Communist Party and quickly rose through its ranks. In 1985, he became party head and, five years later, was elected president of the USSR. As Soviet leader, Gorbachev gained worldwide fame for his program of far-reaching political and economic reforms. He called these reforms perestroika, or "restructuring." Under these reforms, the power of the ruling Communist Party was reduced and there was a new openness, called glasnost. Following the USSR's example, other countries in eastern Europe also called for an end to Communist rule. Gorbachev worked with the United States to reduce the threat of nuclear war and, in 1990, won the Nobel Prize for Peace. In 1991, most of the Soviet republics broke away and formed the Commonwealth of Independent States. Gorbachev then resigned as president and the USSR ceased to exist.

Mikhail Gorbachev with Ronald Reagan in the 1980s

OSAMA BIN LADEN (BORN ca. 1957)

Osama bin Laden is the leader of al-Qaeda, an Islamic terrorist organization based in Afghanistan but with links to other extremist Muslim groups around the world. Born into a wealthy Saudi Arabian family, Bin Laden left in 1979 to fight against the Soviet occupation of Afghanistan. He founded al-Qaeda in the late 1980s. In 1990, Iraq invaded Kuwait and U.S. troops were sent into the region, a move that Bin Laden fiercely opposed. In 1998, he was believed to have been behind the bombing of the U.S. embassies in Kenya and Tanzania. Later he masterminded the horrific terrorist attacks of September 11, 2001, in which some 3,000 people were killed. The United States declared a "war on terror" and demanded Bin Laden's surrender. Despite the continued search, however, Bin Laden has still not been brought to justice.

Bin Laden is believed to be hiding somewhere in the mountains on the border of Afghanistan and Pakistan.

Timeline of Leaders

		Leader	Leadership
ANCIENT	259–210 BC	EMPEROR QIN	Ruler of the Qin dynasty and first emperor of China.
	100–44 BC	JULIUS CAESAR	Roman general who won a civil war and became the dictator of the Roman Republic.
MEDIEVAL/MODERN ERAS	1162–1227	GENGHIS KHAN	Ruler of Mongolia who led Mongol armies in conquests of central Asia.
	1533–1603	ELIZABETH I	Queen of England (1558–1603) who led England to victory against the Spanish Armada.
	1732–1799	GEORGE WASHINGTON	Leader of Americans during the American Revolution; first president of the United States.
	1769–1821	NAPOLEON BONAPARTE	French general who took control of France on two occasions and became emperor of France.
	1809–1865	ABRAHAM LINCOLN	President of the United States (1860–1865) who led the Union in the Civil War; assassinated in 1865.
20TH CENTURY	1878–1953	JOSEPH STALIN	Leading figure in the Russian Revolution and general secretary of the Communist Party who led the Soviet Union in World War II.
	1882–1945	FRANKLIN D. ROOSEVELT	President of the United States (1933–1945) who won four presidential elections.
	1889–1945	ADOLF HITLER	Leader of the German Nazi Party and leader of Germany in World War II.
	1893–1976	MAO ZEDONG	Leader of the Chinese Communist Party, the Long March, and leader of the People's Republic of China (1949–1959).
	1869–1948	MOHANDAS GANDHI	Leader of nonviolent protests for civil rights for Indians and the independence of India from Britain.
	1929–1968	MARTIN LUTHER KING JR.	Leader of civil rights movement in the United States who was assassinated in 1968.
	Born 1931	MIKHAIL GORBACHEV	Head of the Soviet Communist Party and president of the Soviet Union (1990–1991).
	Born 1918	NELSON MANDELA	Leader of the African National Congress in South Africa and president of South Africa (1994–1999).

Consequences

Unified China into a great power.

Unified the Roman Republic, reformed Roman laws, devised the Julian calendar.

Unified the Mongol tribes and built the huge Mongol Empire.

Turned England into a mostly Protestant country and encouraged exploration and trade, which led to the beginnings of the British Empire.

Helped form the United States from a collection of British colonies into an independent nation.

Saved the French Republic from royalists and introduced the Napoleonic Code.

Led the Union to victory against the Confederates in the Civil War and ended slavery.

Transformed the Soviet Union into a powerful nation and killed millions in the Great Purge of political enemies.

Led the Americans out of the Great Depression of the early 1930s and led the United States during World War II.

Expanded Germany by invading other nations and ordered mass murder of Jews.

Founded the People's Republic of China and instituted some policies disastrous for the Chinese.

Improved lives of Indians and helped make India an independent nation in 1947.

Gained better civil rights and voting rights for black Americans.

Introduced political and economic reforms to the Soviet Union and ended the Communist rule of the Soviet Union.

Despite 27 years in prison, helped to rid South Africa of apartheid and established democracy.

Glossary

apartheid (uh-PAHR-tayt) A system of laws in South Africa that divided black and white people from each other and took civil rights away from black people.

civil war (SIH-vul WOR) A conflict between two opposing groups in the same country.

cold war (KOLD WOR) A tense standoff between the Soviet Union and the United States and countries of western Europe, which began after World War II and ended in the 1980s.

communism (KOM-yuh-nih-zem) A political system in which the people own all of a country's property and all work for each other.

displaced (DIS-playst) Expelled or forced to flee from home or homeland.

empire (EM-pyr) A collection of countries or lands ruled by one country.

legion (LEE-jen) A body of about 5,000 Roman soldiers.

monarchy (MAH-nar-kee) A country ruled by a king or queen.

province (PRAH-vins) A part of a country ruled by another country.

racial segregation (RAY-shul seh-grih-GAY-shun) Forcing people of different races to live, work, or go to school separately.

royalists (ROY-uh-lists) People who support a king or queen.

Senate (SEH-nit) The governing body of ancient Rome, which was made up of leading Roman figures.

Index

Web Sites

Due to the changing nature of Internet links, PowerKids Press has developed an online list of Web sites related to the subject of this book. This site is updated regularly. Please use this link to access the list:
www.powerkidslinks.com/topt/leaders/